REPORTING DISTRICT-LEVEL NAEP DATA

SUMMARY OF A WORKSHOP

Committee on NAEP Reporting Practices:
Investigating District-Level and Market-Basket Reporting

Pasquale J. DeVito and Judith A. Koenig, editors

Board on Testing and Assessment

Commission on Behavioral and Social Sciences and Education

National Research Council

NATIONAL ACADEMY PRESS
Washington, D.C.

NATIONAL ACADEMY PRESS 2101 Constitution Avenue, N.W. Washington, D.C. 20418

NOTICE: The project that is the subject of this report was approved by the Governing Board of the National Research Council, whose members are drawn from the councils of the National Academy of Sciences, the National Academy of Engineering, and the Institute of Medicine. The members of the committee responsible for the report were chosen for their special competences and with regard for appropriate balance.

The study was supported by the U.S. Department of Education under contract number E95083001. Any opinions, findings, conclusions, or recommendations expressed in this publication are those of the author(s) and do not necessarily reflect the view of the organizations or agencies that provided support for this project.

International Standard Book Number 0-309-06893-2

Additional copies of this report are available from National Academy Press, 2101 Constitution Avenue, N.W., Washington, D.C. 20418

Call (800) 624-6242 or (202) 334-3313 (in the Washington metropolitan area)

This report is also available online at http://www.nap.edu

Printed in the United States of America

Suggested citation: National Research Council (2000) *Reporting District-Level NAEP Data: Summary of a Workshop.* Committee on NAEP Reporting Practices: Investigating District-Level and Market-Basket Reporting. Pasquale J. DeVito and Judith A. Koenig, editors. Board on Testing and Assessment, Commission on Behavioral and Social Sciences and Education. Washington, DC: National Academy Press.

THE NATIONAL ACADEMIES

National Academy of Sciences
National Academy of Engineering
Institute of Medicine
National Research Council

The **National Academy of Sciences** is a private, nonprofit, self-perpetuating society of distinguished scholars engaged in scientific and engineering research, dedicated to the furtherance of science and technology and to their use for the general welfare. Upon the authority of the charter granted to it by the Congress in 1863, the Academy has a mandate that requires it to advise the federal government on scientific and technical matters. Dr. Bruce M. Alberts is president of the National Academy of Sciences.

The **National Academy of Engineering** was established in 1964, under the charter of the National Academy of Sciences, as a parallel organization of outstanding engineers. It is autonomous in its administration and in the selection of its members, sharing with the National Academy of Sciences the responsibility for advising the federal government. The National Academy of Engineering also sponsors engineering programs aimed at meeting national needs, encourages education and research, and recognizes the superior achievements of engineers. Dr. William A. Wulf is president of the National Academy of Engineering.

The **Institute of Medicine** was established in 1970 by the National Academy of Sciences to secure the services of eminent members of appropriate professions in the examination of policy matters pertaining to the health of the public. The Institute acts under the responsibility given to the National Academy of Sciences by its congressional charter to be an adviser to the federal government and, upon its own initiative, to identify issues of medical care, research, and education. Dr. Kenneth I. Shine is president of the Institute of Medicine.

The **National Research Council** was organized by the National Academy of Sciences in 1916 to associate the broad community of science and technology with the Academy's purposes of furthering knowledge and advising the federal government. Functioning in accordance with general policies determined by the Academy, the Council has become the principal operating agency of both the National Academy of Sciences and the National Academy of Engineering in providing services to the government, the public, and the scientific and engineering communities. The Council is administered jointly by both Academies and the Institute of Medicine. Dr. Bruce M. Alberts and Dr. William A. Wulf are chairman and vice chairman, respectively, of the National Research Council.

COMMITTEE ON NAEP REPORTING PRACTICES: INVESTIGATING DISTRICT-LEVEL AND MARKET-BASKET REPORTING

PASQUALE DeVITO *(Chair)*, Office of Assessment, Rhode Island Department of Education
LINDA BRYANT, Westwood Elementary School, Pittsburgh
C. MELODY CARSWELL, Department of Psychology, University of Kentucky
MARYELLEN DONAHUE, Planning, Research & Development, and District Test Coordination, Boston Public Schools
LOU FABRIZIO, Division of Accountability Services, North Carolina Department of Public Instruction
LEANN GAMACHE, Assessment and Evaluation, Education Services Center, Littleton Public Schools, Littleton, Colorado
DOUGLAS HERRMANN, Department of Psychology, Indiana State University
AUDREY QUALLS, Iowa Testing Program, Iowa City, Iowa
MARK RECKASE, Department of Educational Psychology and Special Education, Michigan State University
DUANE STEFFEY, Department of Mathematical and Computer Sciences, San Diego State University

JUDITH KOENIG, *Study Director*
KAREN MITCHELL, *Senior Program Officer*
KAELI KNOWLES, *Program Officer*
DOROTHY MAJEWSKI, *Senior Project Assistant*

BOARD ON TESTING AND ASSESSMENT

Acknowledgments

At the request of the U.S. Department of Education, the National Research Council (NRC) established the Committee on NAEP Reporting Practices to examine the feasibility and potential impact of district-level and market-basket reporting practices. As part of its charge, the committee sponsored a workshop in September 1999 to gather information on issues related to district-level reporting for the National Assessment of Educational Progress (NAEP). A great many people contributed to the success of this workshop, which brought together representatives from state and local assessment offices, experts in educational measurement, and others familiar with the issues related to district-level reporting for NAEP. The committee would like to thank the panelists and discussants—many of whom traveled to the workshop during a hurricane—for their contributions to a lively and productive workshop. The full participant list appears in Appendix A.

Staff from the National Assessment Governing Board (NAGB), under the leadership of Roy Truby, executive director, and staff from the National Center for Education Statistics (NCES), under the direction of Gary Phillips, acting commissioner, were valuable sources of information. Sharif Shakrani, Mary Lyn Bourque, and Raymond Fields of NAGB and Arnold Goldstein of NCES provided the committee with important background information on numerous occasions. We also thank Keith Rust of Westat for his valuable information on NAEP sampling methodology.

Special thanks are due to a number of individuals at the National Research Council who provided guidance and assistance at many stages during the organization of the workshop and the preparation of this report. We thank Michael Feuer, director of the Board on Testing and Assessment (BOTA), for his expert guidance and leadership of the project. We are indebted to BOTA staff officer, Karen Mitchell, for her assistance in planning the workshop and writing the report; she was a principal source of expertise in both the substance and process for the workshop. We also wish to thank BOTA staff members Patricia Morison, Alix Beatty, Meryl Bertenthal, Naomi Chudowsky, Viola Horek, and John Shephard for their assistance with this work. Special thanks go to Dorothy Majewski, who capably managed the operational aspects of the workshop and the production of this report. We also thank Christine McShane for her advice on structuring the content of the report, her expert editing of the manuscript, and her deft guidance of the report through the publication process.

The committee is particularly grateful to NRC project staff, Judith Koenig, study director, and Kaeli Knowles, program officer, for their efforts in putting together the workshop and preparing the manuscript. Judith acted as the coordinator of the activities while Kaeli played a major role by contacting workshop participants and discussants, soliciting their involvement, guiding them in developing their presentations, and assisting with the writing.

This report has been reviewed in draft form by individuals chosen for their diverse perspectives and technical expertise, in accordance with procedures approved by the National Research Council's Report Review Committee. The purpose of this independent review is to provide candid and critical comments that will assist the institution in making the published report as sound as possible and to ensure that the report meets institutional standards for objectivity, evidence, and responsiveness to the study charge. The review comments and draft manuscript remain confidential to protect the integrity of the deliberative process.

We wish to thank the following individuals for their participation in the review of this report: Susan A. Agruso, Office of Assessment, South Carolina Department of Education; Jonathan Dings, Director of Assessment, Boulder Valley Public Schools, Colorado; Richard Jaeger, School of Education, University of North Carolina, Greensboro (emeritus); Roderick J.A. Little, Department of Biostatistics, School of Public Health, University of Michigan; William D. Schafer, College of Education, University of Maryland; and Roger Trent, Director of Assessment, Ohio Department of Education. Although the individuals listed above have provided constructive comments and suggestions, it must be emphasized that responsibility for the final content of this report rests entirely with the authoring committee and the institution.

Pasquale J. DeVito, *Chair*
Committee on NAEP Reporting Practices: Investigating District-Level and Market-Basket Reporting

Contents

1

Introduction

The National Assessment of Education Progress (NAEP) has earned a reputation as one of the nation's best measures of student achievement in key subject areas. Since its inception in 1969, NAEP has summarized academic performance for the nation as a whole and, beginning in 1990, for the individual states. Increasingly, NAEP results get the attention of the press, the public, and policy makers. With this increasing prominence have come calls for reporting NAEP results below the national and state levels. Some education leaders argue that NAEP can provide important and useful information to local educators and policy makers. They want NAEP to serve as a district-level indicator of educational progress and call for NAEP results to be summarized at the school district level.

At the same time, others have called for simpler, more intuitive and meaningful reporting of NAEP results. Advisers to the National Assessment Governing Board (NAGB) and the National Center for Educational Statistics (NCES) have proposed the use of market-basket reporting methods as one means to accomplish this. Market-basket reporting would allow results to be reported as percentages of items correct on sets of representative items. As part of their evaluation of NAEP, the National Research Council's Committee on the Evaluation of National and State Assessments of Educational Progress stressed the need for clear and comprehensible reporting metrics that would simplify the interpretation of results and endorsed the concept of market-basket reporting for NAEP (National Research Council, 1999a). Market-basket reporting would provide an easier-to-understand picture of students' academic accomplishments.

In pursuit of improved reporting and use of test results, NAEP's stewards are exploring the feasibility and potential impact of district-level and market-basket reporting practices. Accordingly, at the request of the U.S. Department of Education, the National Research Council established the Committee on NAEP Reporting Practices to examine the feasibility and potential impact of district-level and market-basket reporting practices. Because these two topics are intertwined, the committee is examining them in tandem, focusing first on district-level reporting.

During the course of the study, the committee is seeking to answer the following questions regarding district-level reporting for NAEP:

(1) What are the characteristics of district-level NAEP?
(2) If implemented, what information needs might it serve?
(3) What is the degree of interest in participating in district-level NAEP? What factors would influence interest?
(4) Would district-level NAEP pose any threats to the validity of inferences from national and state NAEP?
(5) What are the implications of district-level reporting for other state and local assessment programs?

To begin to address these questions, the committee convened the Workshop on District-Level Reporting for NAEP on September 16 and 17, 1999. Although this workshop relates to one of the committee's charges, it was not intended to bring closure on issues related to district-level NAEP. The committee's work will continue with a workshop on market-basket reporting in February 2000, and joint consideration of the two issues will be taken up in the final report.

WORKSHOP ON DISTRICT-LEVEL REPORTING

The purpose of the National Research Council's Workshop on District-Level Reporting for NAEP was to explore with various stakeholders their interest in and perceptions regarding the likely impacts of district-level reporting. NCES has, to date, had two experiences with district-level reporting. In 1996, NCES contacted several of the larger school districts in the country to gauge their interest in receiving district-level results. The data collected by these districts could potentially meet the requirements for district-level reporting through augmentation of the state NAEP samples, although there would be a fee associated with the augmentation procedures. In 1998, NCES identified several districts that met the sample size requirements "naturally" as a result of the state NAEP sampling procedures; these districts are referred to as the "naturally occurring districts." Additional details on these experiences with district-level reporting appear in Chapter 2.

The workshop consisted of four panels, each with a specific goal. The opening panel was designed to provide broad context for the two-days of workshop discussions. This panel explored the purposes that district-level reporting might serve, discussed who might use the results and how they might be used, and highlighted the key issues that should be considered. Panelists included two individuals who had earlier authored papers discussing the advantages and disadvantages of "below-state" reporting for NAEP as well as representatives from the Council of Chief State School Officers and the Council of Great City Schools. A representative from a district that would qualify for receiving NAEP results served as the discussant.

The second panel provided an opportunity for the committee and workshop participants to hear several state assessment directors discuss the impact that state NAEP has had on their state and local education policy, instruction, and assessment. The concerns that have been expressed regarding district-level reporting at previous committee meetings and elsewhere parallel those considered when state NAEP was implemented in 1990. Thus, the committee thought it would be useful to reflect on the lessons learned from state NAEP as they consider the likely impact of district-level reporting. The presenters focused on the ways in which state NAEP has affected their assessment and instructional programs, the types of comparisons made between NAEP results and state and local assessment results, and what happens when results from various assessments portray differing pictures of achievement. The states represented on this panel were Colorado, Connecticut, Nevada, and Washington. Steve Dunbar, a member of the National Research Council's earlier Committee on the Evaluation of National and State Assessments of Educational Progress, served as the discussant.

The third panel brought together district and state assessment directors to discuss their interests in district-level results, the types of information district-level NAEP would provide, the ways in which district-level results might be used, factors that would bear on their decisions to participate, and issues regarding who should make participation and score release decisions. This panel had four subpanels: the first three subpanels included representatives from naturally occurring districts; each subpanel paired a district representative with a representative from the respective state assessment office, and each speaker addressed the issues in turn. The final subpanel consisted of representatives from districts that had expressed interest in receiving district-level NAEP data in 1996.

Representatives from NAGB, NCES, and the contracting organizations that work on NAEP (the Educational Testing Service and Westat) sat on the final panel. This panel highlighted the technical issues related to sampling and scoring methodologies for district-level reporting and the policy issues related to participation and reporting decisions. Lauress Wise, also a member of the earlier Committee on the Evaluation of National and State Assessments of Educational Progress, served as the discussant.

The workshop was structured so as to permit considerable discussion by presenters as well as participants, much of which is woven into this summary. Time was allotted for each speaker, and following each presentation, substantial time was devoted to open discussion. In preparation for the workshop, speakers were given sets of questions to address during their presentations and asked to supply written responses in advance.[1] Questions posed to the various panelists are included on the agenda, which appears in Appendix A.

ORGANIZATION OF THIS REPORT

The purpose of this summary is to capture the discussions and major points made during the workshop in order to assist NAEP's stewards in their decision making about implementing below-state reporting and to provide information for those who would make decisions about whether or not to participate. The summary is organized as follows. Chapter 2 provides background information on NCES's past experiences with reporting district-level results, along with a discussion of the benefits associated with and the concerns expressed about the implementation of state NAEP, since

[1]Due to inclement weather (Hurricane Floyd), a number of participants were unable to attend the meeting, although some did participate via speaker phone. Their written responses were used in this summary.

it is expected that these parallel issues related to district-level NAEP. Chapter 3 summarizes the information presented by Panel 2 speakers regarding the impact that state NAEP has had on state and local instruction and assessment programs.

The next two chapters reflect the common themes that emerged from discussions at the workshop. There was considerable overlap in the nature of the comments made across the four workshop panels. Thus, instead of summarizing each panel's discussions separately, we have organized these two chapters around the common issues raised during the workshop. Much of the discussion focused on issues related to comparing results from different districts. Chapter 4 is therefore devoted to the subject of interdistrict comparisons. Chapter 5 highlights participants' comments regarding factors that bear on their interest in district-level data. Issues to consider and resolve are summarized in the Chapter 6. Appendix A contains the workshop agenda and list of participants; Appendix B contains general background information on NAEP.

2

Background

This chapter provides background information on experiences with state NAEP and the reporting of district-level NAEP results. The first section describes some of the concerns expressed during the early implementation stages of state NAEP, discusses findings from initial evaluations of the program, and highlights their relationship to district-level reporting. The second section describes prior experiences NCES has had with reporting district-level results through the Trial District Assessment in 1996 and the reporting of results for naturally occurring districts in 1998.

THE STATE NAEP EXPERIENCE

The Trial State Assessment (TSA) was designed with several purposes in mind: (1) to provide states with information about their students' achievement and (2) to allow states to compare their students' performance with that of other students in the states (National Academy of Education, 1993). Implementation was on a trial basis to allow for congressionally mandated evaluations of the program's feasibility and utility before committing resources to an ongoing state-by-state assessment. Prior to its implementation, a number of concerns were expressed about its possible impact. The text below describes some of these concerns, cites some of the benefits reported in reviews of the TSA, and notes how these concerns relate to district-level NAEP.

Early Concerns About Implementation of State NAEP

Concerns about state NAEP centered around the anticipated uses of state-level data and the consequent effects on test preparatory behaviors. Reporting of national-level results had been regarded as having low stakes, since decisions at the state, district, school, or classroom level could not be based on NAEP reports. National-level data were not being used for accountability purposes, and participants were relatively unaffected by the results. But the provision of state-level data prompted concerns about the effects of increasing the stakes associated with NAEP.

As enumerated by Stancavage et al. (1992:261) in discussing the TSA in mathematics, NAEP's stakeholders asked:

(1) Would the reporting of the NAEP TSA cause local districts and states to change the curriculum or instruction that is provided to students?
(2) Would local or state testing programs change to accommodate NAEP-tested skills, would they remain as they are, or would they simply be pushed aside?
(3) Would any such changes in curriculum or assessment, should they occur, be judged as positive by mathematics educators, and others, or would the changes be viewed as regressive and counter-productive?
(4) Finally, would it be found that the entire NAEP TSA effort had no impact at all and was, therefore, a wasteful expenditure of time and money?

These questions stemmed from concerns about the emphases attached to and the inferences drawn from NAEP results. Increasing the stakes associated with NAEP was seen as a move toward using NAEP results for accountability purposes. It was feared that such uses would degrade the value of the assessment. Koretz (1991:21) warned that higher stakes would bring inappropriate teaching to the test and inflated test scores, adding that NAEP results, so far, had been free from "this form of corruption." While this is an important concern, it should also be noted that when state standards mirror the NAEP frameworks, having schools teach the content and skills assessed by NAEP is a desirable result.

Beaton (1992:14) used the term "boosterism" to describe the activities that might be used to motivate students to do their best for the "state's honor." He suggested that boosterism combined with teaching to the test and "more or less subtle ways of producing higher scores could effect the comparability of state trend data over time," particularly if these practices change or become more effective over time.

Others questioned how the results might be interpreted. For instance, Haertel (1991:436) pointed out that the first sort of questions asked would pertain to which states have the best educational systems, but cautioned that attempts to answer would be "fraught with perils." Haertel continued (p.437):

> [Comparisons] will involve generalizations from TSA exercise pools to a broader range of learning outcomes . . . [Such comparisons] depend on the match between NAEP content and states' own curriculum framework . . . For example, a state pressing to implement the [National Council of Teachers of Mathematics] framework might experience a (possibly temporary) decrease in performance on conventional mathematics problems due to its deliberate decision to allocate decreased instruction time to that type of problem. The 1990 TSA might support the (valid) inference that the state's performance on that type of problem was lagging, but not the (invalid) inference that their overall mathematics performance was lagging.

It was expected that state-to-state comparisons would prompt the press and others to rank states, based on small (even trivial) differences in performance (Haertel, 1991). And, in fact, Stancavage et al. (1992) reported that in spite of cautions by NCES and Secretary Lamar Alexander not to rank states, four of the most influential newspapers in the nation rank-ordered states. In a review of 55 articles published in the top 50 newspapers, they found that state rankings were mentioned in about two-thirds of the articles (Stancavage et al., 1992).

Another set of concerns pertained to the types of inferences that might be based on the background, environmental, and contextual data that NAEP collects. These data provide a wealth of information on factors that *relate* to student achievement. However, the data collection design does not support attributions of cause, nor does it meet the needs of accountability purposes. The design is cross-sectional in nature, assessing different samples of students on each testing occasion. Such a design does not allow for the before-and-after testing required to hold educators responsible for results. Furthermore, correlations of student achievement on NAEP with data about instructional practices obtained from the background information do not imply causal relationships. For example, the 1994 NAEP reading results showed that fourth grade students who received more than 90 minutes of reading instruction a day actually performed less well than students receiving less instruction. Clearly, the low-performing students received more hours of instruction to make up for deficiencies; the extra instruction did not *cause* the deficiencies (Glaser et al., 1997).

Reported Benefits of State NAEP

Despite these concerns about the provision of state-level data, reviews of the TSA have cited numerous benefits and positive impacts of the program. Feedback from state assessment officials indicated that state NAEP has had positive influences on instruction and assessment (Stancavage et al., 1992, 1993; Hartka and Stancavage, 1994; DeVito, 1997). At the time that the TSA was first implemented, many states were in the process of revamping their frameworks and assessments in both reading and mathematics. According to state officials, in states where changes were underway, the TSA served to validate the changes being implemented; in states contemplating changes, the TSA served as an impetus for change.

Respondents to surveys conducted by Hartka and Stancavage (1994) reported that the following changes in reading assessment and instruction were taking place: increased emphasis on higher-order thinking skills; better alignment with current research on reading; development of standards-based curricula; increased emphasis on literature; and better integration or alignment of assessment and instruction. While these changes could not be directly attributed to the implementation of the TSA, they reflected priorities set for the NAEP reading assessment. Additionally, many state assessment measures were expanded to include more open-ended response items, with an increased emphasis on the use of authentic texts and passages, like those found on NAEP (Hartka and Stancavage, 1994).

At the time of the first TSA, the new mathematics standards published by the National Council of Teachers of Mathematics (NCTM) were having profound effects on mathematics curricula, instructional practice, and assessment throughout the country. Survey results indicated that changes similar to those seen for reading were happening in mathematics instruction and assessment: alignment with the NCTM standards, increased emphasis on higher-order thinking skills and problem solving, development of standards-based curricula, and integration or alignment of assessment and instruction (Hartka and Stancavage, 1994). The mathematics TSA was also influential in "tipping the balance in favor of calculators (in the classroom and on assessments) and using sample items [for] teacher in-service training" (Hartka and Stancavage, 1994:431). Again, while these changes could not be attributed to the TSA, the fact that the NAEP mathematics frameworks were highly aligned with the NCTM standards served to reinforce the value of the professional standards.

Results from the first TSA in 1990 garnered much attention from the media and the general public. For states whose performance was unsatisfactory, TSA results were helpful in spurring reform efforts. For states that had performed well on TSA, state officials could attribute the results to the recent reforms in their instructional practice and assessment measures.

Relation to District-Level NAEP

It appears from the reviews of the TSA that the expected negative consequences of state NAEP did not materialize and that positive impacts were realized. However, the move to reporting data for school districts brings the level of reporting much closer to those responsible for instruction. As the level of reporting moves to smaller units, the assessment stakes become even higher. Concerns similar to those described above for state-level data have been articulated for below-state reporting (Haney and Madaus, 1991; Selden, 1991; Beaton, 1992; Roeber, 1994). Haney and Madaus (1991) also caution that provision of district-level data could result in putting districts or schools into receivership; using results in school choice plans; or allocating resources on the basis of results. Furthermore, Selden (1991) points out that use of NAEP results at the district or school level has the potential to: discourage states' and districts' use of innovation in developing their own assessments; interfere with the national program with respect to test security—that is, keeping items secure would be more difficult and many new items would be needed; and increase costs in order to accomplish its goals. It will be important to keep these issues in mind as district-level NAEP is being considered.

EXPERIENCES WITH DISTRICT-LEVEL NAEP

The Improving America's Schools Act of 1994, which reauthorized NAEP in that year, modified the policies that guide NAEP's reporting practices. This legislation removed the language prohibiting "below-state" reporting of NAEP results. One means for providing below-state results is through summarizing performance at the school district level. The initiative for providing below-state reporting was supported by the National Assessment Governing Board (NAGB) in the hope that school districts would choose to use NAEP data to inform a variety of education reform initiatives at the local level (National Assessment Governing Board, 1995a). During the 1996 and 1998 administrations of NAEP, different procedures for offering district-level NAEP data to districts and states were explored. The two plans, the Trial District Assessment offered in 1996 and the Naturally-Occurring District plan offered in 1998, are described below.

Trial District Assessment

Under the Trial District Assessment, large school districts were offered three options for participating in district-level reporting of NAEP (National Center for Educational Statistics, 1995a). The first option, called "Augmentation of State NAEP Assessment," offered district-level results in the same subjects and grades as in state NAEP by augmenting the district's portion of the state NAEP sample. Under this option, districts would add "a few schools and students" to their already selected sample in order to be able to report stable estimates of performance at the district level. According to the National Center for Educational Statistics (NCES), the procedures for augmenting the sample would "minimize the cost of the assessment process," and costs were to be paid by the district.

The second option in 1996, referred to as "Augmentation of National Assessment," would allow for reporting district results in subjects and grades administered as part of national NAEP, by augmenting the number of schools selected within certain districts as part of the national sample. As few schools are selected in any single district for national NAEP, this second option would require most school districts to select "full samples of schools" (National Center for Education Statistics, 1995b:2) in order to meet the sampling requirements and to report meaningful results. The cost for augmenting the national sample would be more substantial than those associated with augmenting the state sample.

If a district selected either of these options, the procedures for sample selection, administration, scoring, analysis, and reporting would follow those established for national or state NAEP, depending on the option selected. And the results would be "NAEP comparable or equivalent."

The third option in 1996, the "Research and Development" option, was offered to districts that might not desire NAEP-comparable or equivalent results but that had alternative ideas for using NAEP items. Alternative usage might be assessing a subject or subjects not being administered by

NAEP at the national or state level; administering only a portion of the NAEP instrument; or including a deviation from standard NAEP procedures. NCES would regard such uses as research and development activities and would not certify the results obtained under this option as NAEP comparable or equivalent.

Prior to the 1996 administrations, NCES (with the assistance of the sampling contractor, Westat) determined that the minimum sampling requirements for analysis and reporting at the district level were 25 schools and 500 assessed students per grade and subject. NCES and the Educational Testing Service (ETS) sponsored a meeting during the annual meeting of the American Educational Research Association, inviting representatives from several of the larger districts in the country. On the basis of conversations at this meeting and further interaction with district representatives, NCES identified approximately 10 school systems that were interested in obtaining NAEP results for their districts. NCES and their contractors held discussions with representatives of these districts. The costs turned out to be much higher than school systems could easily absorb. Due mainly to fiscal concerns, only Milwaukee participated in 1996, with financial assistance from the National Science Foundation. Additional sampling of schools and students was required for Milwaukee to reach the minimum numbers necessary for participation, and they received results only for grade 8.

Naturally Occurring Districts

Prior to the 1998 administrations, NCES and Westat determined that there were six naturally occurring districts. Naturally occurring districts are those that comprise at least 20 percent of their state's sample and thus meet the minimum sampling requirements described above (25 schools and 500 students) as a matter of course. These districts can be thought of as "self-representing in state NAEP samples" (Rust, 1999). The districts that met these guidelines in 1998 were:

- Albuquerque, New Mexico;
- Anchorage, Alaska;
- Chicago, Illinois;
- Christiana County, Delaware;
- Clark County, Nevada; and
- New York City, New York.

In July 1998, NCES contacted representatives from these naturally occurring districts to assess their interest in district-level reports, informing them that such results could be generated at no additional cost to the state or the district. Alaska did not participate in 1998, and Christiana County decided it was not interested. In the cases of New York City and Chicago, the districts did not want the data although the respective states did, thereby creating a conflict. The NAEP State Network, which consists of state assessment directors or their appointed representatives, also voiced concerns about the fairness of making the data available for some districts but not others. NCES did not query Clark County or Albuquerque, or their respective states, as to their interest, since by then the whole idea of district-level reporting was coming into question (Arnold Goldstein, National Center for Education Statistics, personal communication, 1999).

3

NAEP's Influence on State Instructional and Assessment Programs

Currently, most states have established content standards and have developed assessment instruments designed to measure their students' mastery of these standards. These standards and assessment instruments vary greatly from state to state, however (Olson et al., in press), and this variation precludes equitable and credible comparisons of student performance using state assessment results (National Research Council, 1999c). Comparisons are made possible by state NAEP. While participation is voluntary, the majority of states have participated in state NAEP since its implementation.

State NAEP reports results in the same ways as national NAEP (see Appendix B), that is, through summaries of performance for the state as a whole and by demographic and background variables using scaled scores and achievement levels. States' uses of these data and their reasons for participating were studied by DeVito (1997). One of the chief reasons states participate, according to DeVito, is to obtain an external reference point for comparing the results of their own assessments and to enable state-to-state and state-to-national comparisons. Moreover, states reported that they use the results to argue for more rigor in their curricula and standards, to examine curricular strengths and weaknesses relative to testing frameworks, and to study NAEP item formats as exemplars. Many states have adopted the NAEP models for standards-based reporting and use NAEP-like achievement levels.

The committee was interested in hearing firsthand discussion of the uses states make of NAEP data. In soliciting participation for the workshop, the committee sought to identify NAEP-participating states that had experienced changes in educational or assessment policy. For example, California recently altered the state's reading curriculum and teaching practices based in part on their students' low reading performance on state NAEP (Jennings et al., 1997). The committee was interested in hearing about California's experience. Other states identified as changing state policy due to NAEP performance were Delaware, Oregon, North Carolina, South Carolina, and Washington. Officials from Washington and South Carolina were invited and able to attend, and the director of assessment for North Carolina serves on the committee. The committee also sought regional representation in the participants. We identified Colorado, Connecticut, Louisiana, Maryland, and Texas, all states with extensive assessment programs in place. Of these states, officials from Colorado and Connecticut were able to attend.

As the purpose of this panel was to understand NAEP's influence on state instructional and assessment programs, representatives from state assessment offices in Colorado, Connecticut, South Carolina, and Washington were asked to share their experiences on if, and how, state NAEP has affected educational policy, instructional practices, and curricular decisions. Their experiences with their state's participation in state NAEP are included in this chapter; their comments on issues pertaining to district-level reporting of NAEP are incorporated into later chapters.

NAEP FRAMEWORKS GUIDE STATE ASSESSMENTS

A common theme voiced by the four state representatives on the panel was the utilization of NAEP frameworks as a resource during the development of their state curriculum standards and the design of state assessments. For example, Connecticut's reading mastery test is built on aspects of the NAEP reading literacy frameworks. According to Peter Behuniak, Connecticut's director of student assessment and testing, the reading comprehension component of the Connecticut Mastery Test in language arts "directly reflects the philosophy of the NAEP frameworks." Connecticut's reading components include all but the NAEP's personal reflection stance.

NAEP's mathematics frameworks influenced the development of the state of Washington's mathematics standards. A high degree of alignment between state content standards and the NAEP content frameworks adds credibility to the state standards, according to the assessment directors, and facilitates comparisons of student performance. When the results of NAEP and the state assessment are in accord, then the NAEP results lend validity to the state results. All three speakers spoke of the problems that arise when the standards are comparable, but comparisons of student performance on NAEP and state tests are not congruent (Chapter 4 addresses these types of comparisons in depth).

ACHIEVEMENT-LEVEL REPORTING IS INFORMATIVE

Speakers also commented on NAEP's use of achievement levels to summarize performance. Don Watson, acting director of student assessment in Colorado's Department of Education, commented that the achievement levels provide a clearer representation of achievement for the public than is possible with numerical scores. In fact, the achievement-level descriptors were so well received in Colorado that the use of similar descriptors was implemented within the state system.

Robert Silverman, Washington's senior analyst for assessment, noted that reporting of NAEP performance by achievement levels had driven changes in his state's policy as well. Results from a recent NAEP administration revealed that 60 percent of their students performed below the proficient level in reading. State legislators interpreted this finding as meaning that their students lacked essential reading skills and advocated for revisions in the state reading instruction and assessment program. Under the amended system, students take an oral reading test in second grade, which allows for early identification and remediation of reading problems. Low-performing students then receive an individualized reading program designed to improve their reading mastery.

NAEP INCLUSION PROCEDURES SERVE AS MODELS

In designing their assessment systems, states have used the NAEP model for inclusion of students with disabilities or limited English proficiency as a reference point in developing their own inclusion procedures. Watson commented that his state, Colorado, revised its policies on the basis of NAEP guidelines. The role of NAEP as the key indicator of academic achievement of all students across the country means that assessment results must include data gathered from students with disabilities and English-language learners. The accommodations and modifications implemented by state NAEP include large print, Braille, and bilingual test versions, smaller testing settings, and untimed versions.

Although NAEP's inclusion and accommodation policies have served as a model for states in modifying their inclusion and accommodation procedures for students with disabilities and those with limited English proficiency, it should also be noted that some states have broader inclusion policies than NAEP. The difference in state-developed and NAEP-established inclusion policies has caused some students to be included in state testing programs but precluded from participation in NAEP.

NAEP ITEM DESIGN IS INNOVATIVE

Speakers agreed that NAEP has been innovative in the design of test items. The release of NAEP items has been useful in guiding item development for their state assessment measures. For example, the use of performance assessments and constructed response questions in NAEP has led to the inclusion of similarly formatted questions in their state instruments. Furthermore, speakers acknowledged that, in many cases, the research involved in developing NAEP items has been more extensive than is possible within state research divisions. For this reason, speakers indicated that they feel quite comfortable using the NAEP design as a model in developing their state tests.

BACKGROUND AND CONTEXTUAL INFORMATION IS USEFUL

Panelists expressed appreciation for the background and contextual information provided by NAEP, as some states collect limited background information on students and school practices. The student questionnaires provide information beyond race/ethnicity and school attendance to include factors thought to influence academic performance, such as language spoken in the home, study and homework habits, and motivation toward school. The teacher questionnaires include a variety of information, such as the training of the teacher, kind of degree attained, number of years of teaching, the amount of control teachers have over instructional issues, and their instructional practice. This information is useful in studying the relationships between background or environmental factors and performance.

PROBLEMATIC ISSUES ASSOCIATED WITH STATE NAEP

The speakers agreed, and workshop participants concurred, that the time of year NAEP is administered is an issue. NAEP administrations occur between February and April, months when states schedule their assessments. The timing conflict has interfered with some states' participation in state NAEP (e.g., Illinois).

Another concern voiced by the speakers was the desire not to overtest students, since many states currently test students in fourth and eighth grade, as does NAEP. In one instance, Robert Silverman remarked that Washington modified their state testing sequence to accommodate NAEP's schedule; they now assess students in third grade instead of fourth grade.

Speakers also stressed that the staff time commitment required to seek participation from schools is substantial. Some schools are reluctant to participate when they learn that scores for their school will not be provided, commenting that participation is not worth the time and effort required.

4
Comparisons with National Benchmarks: Pros and Cons

When Congress removed the language prohibiting the use of NAEP results below the state level (P.L. 103-382), the National Assessment Governing Board (NAGB) was called on to develop guidelines for the conduct of below-state reporting. Their document (National Assessment Governing Board, 1995a:1) states that "below state NAEP results could provide an important source of data for informing a variety of education reform efforts at the local level." While "reform efforts" are not defined in the NAGB document, presumably such efforts would involve making comparisons of local performance with national, state, and other local results. State NAEP answered the persistent question asked by policy makers, "I know how we're doing on our state test, but how are we doing in comparison to other states?" District-level NAEP results could serve a similar purpose for districts so long as item security is maintained and standardized administration practices are utilized.

Large urban districts often face educational challenges that suburban districts do not have to deal with. Urban districts tend to serve larger populations of children who typically score lower on standardized tests. They have larger populations of poor, immigrant, and unemployed families and larger populations of racial/ethnic minorities—all groups who typically score low (Donahue et al., 1999; Shaughnessy et al., 1997). When state assessment results are released, urban districts are often among the lowest performing (*Education Week*, 1998). Faced by the ever-critical press, district officials may respond by enumerating the many challenges they face in educating their students. Many may believe that they are doing the best they can, given their student populations, but without appropriate comparisons, they cannot validate their arguments. For states that have multiple urban areas with common characteristics, results might be compared across similar districts using state assessments. However, many states do not have multiple urban areas. The most appropriate comparisons might be with other districts like themselves in other states.

Workshop participants reported that one of the most powerful uses of NAEP results is for making comparisons against a high-quality, national benchmark. They identified two broad categories of questions that might be answered by such comparisons:

(1) How does our district compare with others like us? Which districts like ours are doing better than we are? What are districts like ours doing that works well?
(2) How do our NAEP results compare to our local or state assessment results?

Speakers also identified a number of disadvantages and limitations associated with such comparisons. The discussion below attempts to summarize the major points made by the speakers.

COMPARISONS AMONG LIKE DISTRICTS COULD SERVE IMPORTANT PURPOSES

The most common argument made in favor of district-level results was the importance of being able to make comparisons among "like districts." Sharon Lewis, director of research for the Council of Great City Schools, reported that the council recently took an "unprecedented stand" by actively recruiting urban school districts to volunteer to take the proposed voluntary national tests. This action was prompted by council members' desire to know how school districts are doing when measured against high standards and in comparison to other districts with similar characteristics. Lewis noted that urban school districts administer a number of commercially developed tests that allow them to answer questions about how well the district is doing. But these test results do not allow them to compare across districts, particularly to large urban districts in other states.

Other workshop participants echoed the desire for appropriate comparison groups. Thomas McIntosh, representing Nevada's Department of

Education, remarked that comparisons would be useful if the relevant factors that influence performance could be controlled. He highlighted social and economic factors as important ones to be controlled and called for measures based on environment, cultural differences, number of books in the home, and parental expectations in addition to the more common measures based on the percentage of students receiving free and reduced-price lunches in districts. According to McIntosh, comparisons made after controlling for these social and economic factors would be useful in identifying who is doing well and what they are doing that works. He added that there is a need for comparisons that cannot be explained away by factors, such as differences in growth rates, size, or income (e.g., "you can't compare us with them because we're bigger" or ". . . because we're growing faster" or ". . . because they have more money," etc.). He noted that it is very easy to undermine comparisons and offer justifications and rationales for poor achievement. The largest district in his state, Clark County, is quite different from other districts in Nevada.

Gerald DeMauro, New York's coordinator of assessment, agreed, saying that comparisons with like districts are important, but demographic information is needed in order to verify that the comparison is appropriate. The smaller the pool, the more important the characteristics of the pool. For DeMauro, the demographic characteristics of a city and those of a state can be strikingly different. Thus, comparisons of cities or districts that share common characteristics might be more meaningful than comparisons with the state as a whole.

Nancy Amuleru-Marshall, Atlanta's executive director for research and assessment, presented her district's perspective, saying:

> NAEP may represent the best effort so far in the development of rich and meaningful assessments. . . . NAEP would provide districts with high-quality performance data that we currently do not have. It would permit districts to make peer comparisons, as well as state and national comparisons. Many of the districts that are members of the Council of Great City Schools have been struggling to find common measures of student achievement that are valid indicators of our students' performance. NAEP can provide such a measure.

Amuleru-Marshall added that Atlanta was one of the districts that stood behind President Clinton's call for voluntary national testing and has been disappointed that the testing program has not been available to them yet.

Representatives from several state assessment offices also pointed out that the state is ultimately responsible for ensuring that school systems are carrying out their charge of educating the state's youth. An additional measure of the extent to which school systems are doing their jobs would be useful. Moreover, the ability to compare data for their urban districts with those in other states would help them set reasonable expectations for these jurisdictions.

EXTERNAL VALIDATION IS DESIRED

Workshop participants observed that another appealing feature of district-level reporting for NAEP would be the ability to compare district assessment results with stable external measures of achievement. According to Paul Cieslak, research specialist for the Milwaukee Public Schools, NAEP is a "good, well-constructed external validation measure that provides a solid base for longitudinal and out-of-district comparisons." Others pointed out that there had been, and continue to be, revisions in their state assessment programs. NAEP remains consistent from one testing interval to the next, which makes it useful for providing trend data that are not possible with a changing state assessment system.

COMPARISONS CAN HAVE NEGATIVE CONSEQUENCES

A number of district representatives disagreed with the views that comparisons of like districts would provide useful information. They countered that large urban districts already know from currently administered tests that their students perform poorly on standardized assessments. They do not need to see themselves compared with another district in order to know this. "We already know we're not doing well," commented one district representative, "and another test on which we would score low would only fuel the fire for those more than ready to criticize us."

Others added that districts have limited resources available, asking "Would district-level reporting be a good use of limited district resources?" They questioned whether the benefits would justify the costs, commenting that additional testing would consume instructional time and would utilize district funds.

CONTEXT FOR TESTING VARIES ACROSS STATES

Behuniak (Connecticut) pointed out another drawback with comparisons across state boundaries—while districts may seem comparable based on their demographics, they may in fact be very different due to being located in a certain state. The state sets the context and the environment within which testing occurs. States differ in the emphases they place on test results, the uses of the scores, and the amounts and kinds of attention results receive from the press. These factors play a heavy role in setting the stage for the testing. Attempts to make comparisons across like districts need to consider the context for testing along with similarities in student populations.

COMPARISONS CAN CREATE A DOUBLE BIND

Speakers noted that attempts to obtain external validation can create a double bind. When the findings from external measures corroborate state assessment results, no questions are asked. However, when state or local assessment results and external measures (such as state NAEP) differ, assessment directors find themselves being asked, "Which set of results is correct?" Explaining and accounting for these differences can be challenging. One state assessment representative indicated that when state results are higher than NAEP results, he emphasizes the alignment of the state assessment with the curriculum. When state results are lower than NAEP, he points out that the state standards are higher.

Some state assessment programs have adopted the NAEP descriptors (advanced, proficient, and basic) for their achievement levels. However, their descriptions of performance differ in important ways from the NAEP descriptions. NAEP's definition of "proficient," for instance, may encompass different skills than the state's definition of proficient. This difference creates problems for those who must explain and interpret the two sets of test results.

In addition, confusion arises when NAEP results are released at the same time as state or local assessment results. State and local results are timely, generally reporting data for a cohort while it is still in the particular grade. For instance, when reports are published on the achievement of a school system's fourth graders, they represent the cohort *currently* in fourth grade. When NAEP results are published, they are for some *previous* year's fourth graders. Users of the data (policy makers, the press, etc.) may attempt to compare cohorts across assessments, but when they realize that the results are for different cohorts, attention focuses on the more recent results; NAEP results may be dismissed. This time lag in reporting affects the extent to which NAEP can be a catalyst for change at the local level.

5
Factors That Influence Interest In District-Level NAEP

Recent federal initiatives reflect the desires of national policy makers to be able to compare student achievement levels with national benchmarks and to attempt to verify the rigor of state and local standards. President Clinton's call for the voluntary national tests in reading and mathematics is one example; the tests' design would strive to create individual measures linked to NAEP to the maximum extent possible, thereby enabling comparisons of individual performance with national benchmarks. Other examples of the desire for comparable test scores are recent congressional requests for studies on the feasibility of developing equivalency scales in order to "link" scores from commercially available standardized tests and state assessments to each other and to NAEP (National Research Council, 1999c) and on the feasibility of embedding common sets of test questions into state and local assessments in order to obtain common measures of individual achievement (National Research Council, 1999b).

Thus, it seems clear that the desire for a means of comparing achievement across jurisdictions as well as with national indicators originates within the highest policy-making levels in this country. And while federal policy makers make the decisions regarding such programs, they are not the ones immediately affected. Those most closely affected are students and their families, educators, and administrators at the local and state level. The workshop sought to hear from representatives from state and local assessment offices, the individuals who would be expected to handle such programs.

Workshop Panel 3 was intended to get at the issues that bear on states' and districts' interest in district-level reporting. Panelists responded to questions posed to them in advance (see Appendix A), and their responses are incorporated into the discussion that follows. As the committee listened to participants interact with each other throughout the two days, it became clear that the questions served as a springboard for further discussion. While some were answered quickly, others stimulated lengthy discussion and were addressed by more than one panel. The text below attempts to capture these discussions and highlight the issues that seemed most important to panelists.

WHAT ARE THE GOALS AND OBJECTIVES OF DISTRICT-LEVEL NAEP?

A Hammer in Search of a Nail

Several participants felt that the proposal for district-level NAEP is like a hammer searching for a nail. They commented that national NAEP and state NAEP are designed with specific goals in mind, and they serve their purposes well. But, as stated by one participant, "one size does not fit all," and the goals and objectives set for national and state NAEP are not necessarily suitable for district-level reporting. They commented that it was hard to respond to the questions put to them in preparation for the workshop without knowing the sponsors' and others' objectives for district-level assessment.

Workshop participants maintained that school systems typically use test results to modify and improve instruction. According to Sharon Lewis, representing the Council of Great City Schools: "When schools use assessments to improve the quality of the education offered in their schools, they analyze and use test . . . results to change behaviors. They follow a cycle of teaching, testing, modifying instructional practices, developing/purchasing appropriate materials, and then repeat the cycle—teach, test, modify, etc.– hoping to see results." Several speakers questioned whether NAEP results would fit with these purposes, commenting that decisions based on assessment data are made at the individual, classroom, or school level, not at the district level.

Speakers further noted that, in their localities, tests are typically used for accountability purposes and are often associated with high stakes. NAEP, they argued, is not designed as an accountability tool or to yield causal inferences regarding achievement, relationships with curricula, or other factors. The frameworks are not necessarily aligned with local curricula, and using NAEP scores to evaluate schools and teaching practices would be neither appropriate nor informative. Using NAEP for the purpose of making high-stakes decisions might also degrade its ability to provide the independent monitoring information it has been designed to provide. When high stakes are attached to test results, motivation to do well increases. Motivation can result in improved teaching practices that lead to actual improvements in skill levels, or motivation can prompt the use of unacceptable test preparation methods that serve to increase test scores without commensurate improvements in the tested knowledge and skills.

A clear message from the participants was that their interest in district-level results would rely on details about the program. They encouraged NAEP's stewards to develop explicit statements of the goals and objectives to be accomplished by district-level results.

Providing Information Not Currently Available

As noted above, most states currently administer state-developed assessments as well as commercially available tests (Olson et al., in press). Workshop participants told the committee they might welcome additional assessments that serve new and useful purposes, such as allowing comparisons among like districts in other states, as noted earlier. However, they emphasized that a substantial amount of time is currently devoted to testing.

Several speakers began their talks by listing the tests currently administered to their students. The remarks of these speakers are presented below to exemplify the extent of testing currently done in the jurisdictions represented at the workshop. According to Judy Costa, testing director for Nevada's Clark County School District:

> In the fall, we administer the CTBS/5 or TerraNova to our fourth grade students as well as the TCS/2, which is a test of "school ability," in addition to a state-mandated direct writing assessment. In the spring, we administer a series of district-developed curriculum-based criterion-referenced tests in reading, mathematics, and language arts.
>
> At the middle school level, the eighth grade schedule is similar to that for fourth grade, although the curriculum-based criterion-referenced tests are still in the process of development and will be piloted this spring and administered in earnest next year.

> At grade 11, we administer state-developed criterion-referenced tests in reading and mathematics, with science and social studies to be added shortly, as well as a direct writing assessment. These tests are taken as part of a certification for graduation process. Eleventh-grade students who do not pass these graduation tests must take them again in twelfth grade, until they finally pass. Unsuccessful students will have up to eight opportunities in eleventh and twelfth grade to pass these tests. In addition to the graduation tests, we administer the CTBS/5 and the TCS/2 to all students in grade 12 and on an optional basis at grade 11. Please notice that additional testing is conducted at other grades, but I have only highlighted the NAEP grade levels.

This amount of testing is not unique to Clark County. Students in Chicago take: the Iowa Test of Basic Skills (optional in grades 1 and 2 but required in grades 3 though 8); the Iowa Test of Basic Skills achievement tests in grades 9 and 10; performance assessments in K-2, currently optional at the school level, but close to being required in some areas; the Test of Achievement and Proficiency in high school; the PLAN published by ACT, Inc.; semester exams in grade 11 in English, mathematics, science, and social studies; the Illinois state assessments in reading, mathematics, and writing in third, fifth, and eighth grades, and in science and social studies for grades 4 and 7; and the Prairie State Achievement Test in grade 11. In fact, the Illinois teachers union became sufficiently concerned about the amount of time devoted to testing that they moved to have limits set. Students in Illinois are now limited to a maximum of 25 hours of state-initiated testing during the K-12 years. Local assessment is not subject to the 25-hour limit and is regarded as the most important tool for improving curriculum and instruction.

The state assessment program in Georgia is also quite comprehensive. According to Amuleru-Marshall, Atlanta's program includes a structured assessment in kindergarten; norm-referenced tests in grades 3, 5, and 8; newly developed criterion-referenced tests in grades 4, 6, and 8; and a series of high school graduation tests in language arts, writing, mathematics, science, and social studies for eleventh graders.

The school district of Philadelphia is developing an assessment system that includes a national norm-referenced exam (Stanford Achievement Test, Ninth Edition); citywide end-of-course exams in English, mathematics, science, and social studies for grades 7-12; and a K-4 system of curriculum-embedded and on-demand assessments of literacy and mathematics. In addition, the state annually administers reading, mathematics, and writing assessments.

Given the extensive amount of testing already occurring in their school systems, workshop participants contended that the introduction of new testing would have to be associated with useful, unique, and timely information. District NAEP would need to be designed to meet needs not served by tests already in place in jurisdictions.

Several speakers suggested that the introduction of district NAEP might serve to increase participation in state and national NAEP. They maintained that, currently, school districts have little motivation to participate in the national and state programs, since they receive no feedback on their performance. Yet the integrity of NAEP results depends on sufficient and accurate participation at the school level. Providing feedback to school districts may increase interest and raise participation rates in the state and national programs. Remarks by Paula Mosley, coordinator of student testing and evaluation for the Los Angeles Office of Instruction, elucidate this position:

> District scores would provide an incentive for the students, teachers, and administrative staff involved in the NAEP testing. Currently, it is difficult to get schools to participate because they know there are no [below-state] reports provided. A greater "buy-in" by the stakeholders affected may [occur] if they knew they were representing the district. Schools, administrators, teachers, and students [sacrifice instructional and planning time] to administer NAEP. They should receive feedback for their efforts.

Some participants agreed with Mosley, stressing that if they were to advocate for participation in NAEP, their schools and teachers would need to receive something in exchange for their efforts—preferably something not available from current programs.

Others were hesitant to agree that simply providing new and unique information would be enough to elicit higher participation rates in state or national NAEP. They claimed that increased participation in a program comes with increased involvement in the program. When state and local officials seek to "win over" teachers and administrators, they search for ways to include educators in activities such as test development and scoring. They find that this type of involvement influences educators' depth of understanding and motivation to accomplish objectives, asserting that "when teachers are involved in creating the test, they understand what they have created, and they feel ownership of results."

Workshop participants questioned whether NAEP's stewards would be able to motivate teachers and administrators to buy into NAEP, since they would feel little ownership of the program. They felt that additional reporting feedback would probably not be likely to increase motivation to participate. Furthermore, some participants would not consider district NAEP useful without school and student scores that could be clearly linked to curriculum and instruction.

Assessments in Additional Subject Areas and Grades

Workshop participants were intrigued by the possibility of having assessments in areas they would not normally test. For instance, the speakers from Illinois found the NAEP assessments in foreign language and fine arts to be appealing. Amuleru-Marshall agreed, stating that in Atlanta, content and performance standards are being developed for grades 3, 5, 8, and 10 in language arts, mathematics, science, social studies, fine arts, foreign language, and health and physical education. However, development has slowed due to cost issues, and only the language arts and mathematics assessments have moved forward. NAEP assessments could be used in place of locally developed assessments or until such tests are ready.

Amuleru-Marshall also remarked that if NAEP results were available, Atlanta could justify eliminating some of the existing assessments and would also have new data in multiple content areas. Harry Selig, a research manager with the Houston Independent School District, observed that making NAEP assessments available has the potential for allowing districts to "refrain from conducting current norm-referenced testing." Selig added that using NAEP assessments could reduce their testing costs and lessen the fatigue effects on students due to extensive testing.

Speakers noted that the subject areas tested by *state* NAEP (e.g., reading, writing, mathematics, and science) are, for the most part, already tested by state assessments. Their desire would be for quality assessments in other areas, such as those tested on *national* administrations of NAEP. They wondered which assessments would be made available.

Speakers had varying opinions about the grade levels covered by the national assessments. National NAEP currently provides assessments in three grades: fourth, eighth, and twelfth; state NAEP offers assessments in fourth and eighth grades. Both assess students biennially. Several speakers mentioned that additional information on twelfth graders would be an appealing feature of district-level NAEP scores.

The sparsity of grade levels represented was cited by others as a shortcoming. As noted above, school systems use assessment findings for accountability purposes and to improve teaching practices. Indicators of performance at only three grades would not allow for tracking achievement across grades, since off-grade-level assessments would be missing. Nor would testing in one elementary grade, one middle school grade, and one high school grade every two years prove useful. While this cycle of testing serves the purposes of providing national indicators of performance, it would not meet the needs of districts and school systems, according to the workshop participants.

Comparisons Over Time

Participants expressed interest in the prospect of being able to make comparisons over time based on district-level NAEP data. However, they also recognized that a number of factors might affect the stability of results, making comparisons over time less meaningful. Whereas state boundaries are fixed, school district boundaries change. Schools may be moved from one district to another; new housing developments may alter the characteristics of the student population. With small sample sizes, slight alterations in the composition of a district could have large effects on results. Factors unrelated to student achievement levels, such as changes in inclusion rules for students with disabilities or students with limited English proficiency, or changes in motivation to do well on standardized tests, could produce differences in performance.

Comparisons Over Groups

Many participants commented about the usefulness of the NAEP background, contextual, and environmental data. They were interested in obtaining this information about their students and alluded to examining score data by population subsets. However, it was not clear whether any districts would have sufficient numbers of test takers to allow this level of reporting.

WHO WOULD BE ELIGIBLE TO PARTICIPATE?

Proposed Sampling Design for Districts

In preparation for the workshop, the National Center for Education Statistics (NCES) and Westat provided two documents as background material on sampling issues that outlined the proposed sampling plans for district-level reporting (Rust, 1999; National Center for Education Statistics, 1995b). For state NAEP, the sample design involves two-stage stratified samples. Schools are selected at the first stage, and students are selected at the second stage. The typical state sample size is 3,000 sampled students per grade and subject, with 30 students per school. The sample sizes desired for district results would be roughly one-quarter that required for states (750 sampled students at 25 schools to yield 500 participants at 25 schools). This sample size would be expected to produce standard errors for districts that are about twice the size of standard errors for the state.

According to the information provided, a district that wishes to report subgroup mean proficiencies for a large number of subgroups—such as race, ethnicity, type of courses taken, home-related variables, instructional variables, and teacher variables—would need sample sizes approximately one-half of its corresponding state sample size, approximately 1,500 students from a minimum of 50 schools. For reporting, the "rule of 62" would apply, meaning that disaggregated results would be reported only for cell sizes with at least 62 students (National Assessment Governing Board, 1995b: Guideline 3).

At the workshop, Richard Valliant, associate director of Westat's Statistical Group, provided additional details on sampling requirements for districts. Valliant described the "sparse state" option, which would require fewer schools but would sample more students at the selected schools. The "small state" option would reduce the number of students per school. Both options still require 500 tested (participating) students. These sample sizes would allow for the reporting of proficiencies (or scaled scores), achievement levels, and percentages of students at or above a given level for the entire district, but would probably not allow for stable estimates of performance for subsets of the sample.

Peggy Carr, associate commissioner in the Assessment Division at NCES, described two additional alternatives being considered for future assessments, the "enhanced district sampling plan" and the "analytic approach." The enhanced district sampling plan would reconfigure the state sampling design so that sufficient numbers of schools were sampled for interested districts. This plan might require oversampling at the district level and the application of appropriate weights to schools, and perhaps districts, during analysis.

The analytic approach, according to Carr, would allow districts to access existing data in order to identify districts like themselves and compare results analytically. Carr noted that development of details about this option is still under way.

Serving Small Districts

Workshop participants expressed concern about the sampling requirements. These requirements mean that a district needs at least 25 schools with a given grade level in order to receive reports (e.g., to receive results for eighth graders, the district needs to have at least 25 middle schools). While NCES and the National Assessment Governing Board (NAGB) did not provide an estimate of the number of districts that might qualify, several speakers offered estimates. Lauress Wise, president of the Human Resources Research Organization, distributed a handout showing that about 400 of the 16,000 districts in the country have at least 25 schools. According to Wise's handout, 170 districts have between 20 and 24 schools with total student populations of size 6,000 or more, and 441 districts have 25 or more schools with total student populations of at least 6,000. Wise noted that his data did not provide breakdowns by grade level. Wayne Martin, director of the State Education Assessment Center of the Council of Chief State School Officers, provided a by-grade estimate for fourth grade. According to Martin's estimate, approximately 300 school districts would have sufficient numbers of students in the fourth grade to meet the criteria.

The proposed sampling criteria prompted comments regarding the intent of district-level reporting. Participants questioned whether the intent was to make district-level results available to *all* districts or only to *large urban* districts. Martin recounted his conversations with state representatives at the recent NAEP State Network meeting:

> When I asked how they might feel if results were only generated for the large school districts, a number of states suggested that this would create a different set of problems . . . [C]harges of favoritism could lead to . . . cooperation problems with smaller districts [in state and national NAEP], whereas being singled out could further exacerbate differences between the state agency and large districts.

Participants wondered how many districts nationally would meet these requirements and asked about the definition of a "district." Several questioned whether district consortia would be allowed. In connection with the Third International Mathematics and Science Survey, a group of districts in Illinois formed a consortium in order to participate and receive results. They asked whether such a consortium would be allowed for NAEP.

Wise asked if NCES and Westat had thoroughly considered the difference between district and state- and national-level sampling issues in conjunction with the accuracy of results. In state and national NAEP, there is considerable variation in average achievement levels across schools, and only a small percentage of schools are sampled and tested. A target of 100 different schools was set to be sure that the between-school variation was adequately captured. In district NAEP, there would be far fewer schools and also less variability between schools. In smaller districts, all schools might be tested, eliminating completely the portion of sampling error associated with between-school differences. Wise advised NCES and Westat to further pursue this issue, focusing on the estimated overall accuracy of results rather than specifying an arbitrary minimum number of schools.

Acceptance of Sampling Designs

Although they make use of results from national and state NAEP samples, educators and politicians may lack confidence in survey-based results at the district level; they may instead want information based on a full census. NAEP employs complex sampling designs for students and questions. Speakers from Colorado and Illinois, for instance, commented that their legislators may question the legitimacy of test results based on samples.

Watson noted that an assessment program in Colorado, designed to employ sampling, was within weeks of being implemented when the state withdrew support. The then-current design of the Colorado State Assessment Program called for assigning schools to one of three content areas being assessed (reading, writing, and geography). All students at the identified grade were to be tested in only that content area. Students and schools were to receive results based on the area in which they were tested. The district was to receive information across all areas, under the assumption that the sampling was sufficient to provide dependable district-level information. These plans were communicated and materials were ready for printing for a March/April administration, when the legislation was changed to eliminate all sampling.

Workshop speakers from Illinois added that their testing programs that use samples have been changed. Other participants agreed that NAEP's designs for sampling students and test questions may be difficult to sell at the local level.

HOW MUCH WOULD DISTRICT-LEVEL NAEP COST?

Under the 1996 augmentation options described earlier in this report, districts were given the opportunity to augment their state samples to obtain district-level results. Although a number of districts were initially interested in this plan, nearly all dropped out because of the projected expense. Only Milwaukee participated, and the costs were covered by a National Science Foundation grant.

Workshop participants had questions about who was to pay for the costs of participating: Would any of the costs be paid for by the federal government? Were the districts and states to assume responsibility for the costs? Would districts and states be expected to provide staff to handle the administrations? They commented that in order to obtain funding, they would need to convince legislators and policy makers of the potential benefits. Panelists recommended that NAGB and NCES examine the various components of the costs, identify the features associated with higher costs, and consider modifying procedures in order to reduce costs.

WHAT PRODUCTS WOULD DISTRICT-LEVEL NAEP GENERATE AND WHEN WOULD THEY BE RELEASED?

Characteristics of Reports

Questions arose as to the nature of the information that would be provided to states and districts. Would they receive a formal report, like those prepared as part of the existing NAEP program? Would the report contain explanatory information that would help users interpret the results? Participants commented that the types of reports currently provided as part of NAEP are considered both attractive and useful.

In contrast, the sample report included in the materials supplied by NCES was simply a computer printout of information (National Center for Education Statistics, 1995b). Some held that it would be difficult to sell participation to policy makers if in exchange for their efforts (and money) they would only receive computer printouts. Others wondered if they would receive electronic data files to use in producing their own reports. They realized that NAEP makes use of complex procedures in order to produce performance estimates (i.e., the conditioning process and plausible values technology). They wondered if they would be expected to implement this technology and produce their own reports.

Overall, they felt that a prototype report was needed to exemplify the type of information that would be provided about districts. A prototype report would enable policy makers to make participation decisions based on the type and usefulness of information they would receive.

Length of Time for Reporting Results

Workshop participants also posed questions about the length of time it would take to receive the reports. The time delay currently seen for the release of NAEP results is between 12 and 18 months. For assessments useful in instructional planning and monitoring, school districts are accustomed to receiving test results within six weeks of the administration; in fact, some results are ready within one week of testing (Chicago). The current time lag for receiving reports would seriously degrade the usefulness of NAEP data for districts, and speakers questioned what they would legitimately be able to do with the data. By the time results were received, the students in the grades tested would have moved on to the next grade. What inferences could be made from the results, and how would they be applied?

Conditioning and Plausible Values Technology

Nancy Allen, director of NAEP analysis and research at the Educational Testing Service, presented an overview of the procedures used to generate group-level results. Allen reminded participants that ability estimates are not computed for individuals, due to the fact that any one student responds to too few items to produce reliable estimates of performance. She described procedures used to generate the likely ability distributions for individuals, based on their background characteristics and responses to cognitive items (the conditioning procedures), and to randomly draw five ability estimates (plausible values) from these distributions. She noted that for state NAEP, the conditioning procedures utilize information on the characteristics of all test takers in the state.

Questions arose as to what information would be included in the conditioning models for districts. Would the models be based on the characteristics of the state or the characteristics of the district? To what extent would model misspecification lead to bias in the estimates? Allen responded that the conditioning models rely on information about the relationships between performance on test items and background characteristics. Sometimes the *compositional characteristics* of the state and a district will differ, based on background data, but the *relationships* between cognitive performance and background characteristics may not differ. Nevertheless, Allen stressed that they were still exploring various models for calculating estimates at the district level.

Participants remarked that it was important to resolve these issues because of the associated expenses and/or time delays in finalizing results that they create. Wise questioned the extent of the conditioning needed. He commented that if district-level reports did not include disaggregated data (due to the rule of 62 for reported cells), the conditioning might not need to include all background variables.

WHO WOULD MAKE PARTICIPATION DECISIONS? WHO WOULD OWN THE DATA?

Roy Truby, executive director of the National Assessment Governing Board, told participants that when Congress lifted the ban on below-state reporting, it neglected to include language in the law that clarified the roles of states and districts in making participation decisions. In 1998, when NCES offered results to the naturally occurring districts, letters were sent to the districts and their respective states. Based on legal advice from the Department of Education's Office of General Counsel, state officials would make the decision on release, not the district. In one case, there appeared to be a conflict in which the state wanted the data released, but the district did not.

Original policy provided that the district-level results would be made available only with the district's approval. Upon advice from the Office of General Counsel, the policy was changed to provide that states must give permission for the release of district data from state NAEP samples, but that states should be encouraged to consult with the districts involved before deciding. NAGB members were concerned that the districts were not told when they agreed to participate in 1998 NAEP that scores for their districts might be produced. Because of this ambiguity about decision-making procedures, NAGB passed the following resolution (National Assessment Governing Board, 1999):

> Since the policy on release of district-level results did not envision a disagreement between state and district officials, the Governing Board hereby suspends implementation of this policy, pending legislation which would provide that the release of district-level NAEP results must be approved by both the district and state involved.

In preparation for the workshop, participants had been asked their opinions about which entity, the state or the district, should have the ultimate decision-making authority regarding participation and release of data.

In general, district representatives believed that the participating entity should make participation decisions, while state representatives believed that the decision should lie with the state. Some added that the entity that paid for participation should have the ultimate decision-making authority. However, the overarching issue related to *release* of the results. Under the Freedom of Information Act, once results for districts are produced, they are subject to release to the public. Speakers stressed that the issue was not so much about *participation* as about the fact that once the district had participated, the results would have to be released to the public upon request.

6
Summing Up: Issues to Consider and Resolve

One of the intended goals of the workshop was to highlight factors that would affect states' and districts' interest in having district-level results. While no attempt was made to establish consensus about any of the suggestions that were made, several themes emerged from the interactions among workshop participants. The following discussion points out issues that need to be considered and resolved before implementation decisions can be made.

CLARIFY THE GOALS AND OBJECTIVES

The goals of district-level reporting for NAEP were not apparent to workshop participants. Some spoke of using tests for accountability purposes, pondering whether NAEP could be used in this way or not. They discussed the amount of testing currently done in their schools and stressed that new testing would need to be accompanied by new (and better) information. However, some had trouble identifying what new and better information might come from district-level NAEP data. Their comments might have been different, and perhaps more useful, if they had a clear idea of the purposes and objectives for district-level reporting. It would be helpful to have an explicit statement of the goals and objectives for district-level reporting combined with a logical argument for how the program is expected to achieve the desired outcomes.

DEVELOP SPECIFICATIONS

There were varying understandings among the participants about the nature and characteristics of district-level reporting. Participants talked about the possibility of receiving information that is currently part of national NAEP, commenting that the breadth of content areas and grades tested were attractive features. Some discussed receiving school-level or individual-level scores. Others generated their own assumptions in order to respond to the questions posed to them. One speaker stated his self-formulated assumptions then noted that if any of the assumptions proved to be inaccurate, "my testimony would change accordingly."

Many speakers highlighted background data as being very useful and were intrigued by the prospect of seeing performance data broken down by background characteristics. Speakers were not aware that given the sample sizes required, such information is not likely to be provided. Their comments suggest the need for clear statements on the specifications for and constraints on district-level reporting.

EVALUATE COSTS AND BENEFITS

What would districts and states receive? When would they receive the information? How much would it cost? What benefits would be realized from the information? Workshop participants responded to questions about their interests in the program without having answers to these questions. Nonetheless, many said that their interest would depend on the answers. They need information on the types of reports to be prepared—a prototype report would be very useful for this—and the associated costs. Would there be varying levels of expense depending on the nature of the report?

Very important to the participants would be the time lag in receiving reports. Would they receive information in time to use it in their decision and policy making? Or would the time delays be such as to render the information useless? Are there options for reports that would require less preparation time?

In addition to monetary concerns, the costs in terms of time and effort on the part of teachers and students must also be considered. School systems already extensively test fourth and eighth graders. If more time is to be taken away from instruction for the purpose of additional testing, the benefits of the testing need to be laid out. Will additional testing amplify the information already provided? Or will the information be redundant to that provided from current tests? Will the redundancy make it useful for external validation? Such information is important if NAEP's stewards want to assess actual levels of interest.

EVALUATE PARTICIPATION LEVELS

Many speakers talked of the value of being able to make interdistrict comparisons based on districts with like characteristics. However, this use of the results rides on the assumption that sufficient numbers of districts will participate. Previous experiences with district-level reporting resulted in between 10 and 12 interested districts in 1996 and virtually no interested districts in 1998.

Meaningful comparisons, as defined by demographic, political, and other contextual variables that districts believe are important, depend on there being a wide variety of other districts with district-level reports. Having only a handful of districts that meet the sampling criteria may limit one of the most fundamental functions for district-level reporting, that is, having a carefully selected group of other districts against which to compare results. Thus, if making comparisons is the primary objective for receiving district-level reports, the targeted districts must feel secure in knowing that there are sister districts also completing the necessary procedures for receiving district-level results. The extent of participation will limit the ability to make the desired comparisons.

CONSIDER WAYS TO SERVE SMALL DISTRICTS

According to the sampling criteria, participation would be limited because many districts would not qualify to receive reports. However, if having district-level data turns out to be associated with educational improvements, should small districts be denied access to such an important program? The Third International Mathematics and Science Survey (TIMSS) has permitted a district consortium for the most recent assessment. Would such consortia be allowed for NAEP reporting, and would the reports be meaningful to the participants? If credible results are to be provided for all individual districts, would this necessitate implementing district NAEP as a census rather than a sample? These are issues that NAEP's stewards need to address as they consider the goals, objectives, specifications, and components for district-level reporting.

CONSIDER THE IMPACT OF RAISING THE STAKES

A concern expressed when state NAEP was first implemented related to the increased stakes that would be associated with reporting data for smaller units. The message from several speakers (particularly district representatives) was that district-level reports would raise the stakes associated with NAEP. An evaluation of the effects of higher stakes, particularly as they relate to the types of inferences that may be made, would be important.

References

Beaton, A.E.

1992 Methodological Issues in Reporting NAEP Results at District and School Levels. Paper commissioned by the National Assessment Governing Board.

DeVito, Pasquale J.

1997 The future of the National Assessment of Educational Progress from the states' perspective. In *Assessment in Transition: Monitoring the Nation's Educational Progress.* Stanford, CA: National Academy of Education.

Donahue, P.L., K.E. Voelkl, J.R. Campbell, and J. Mazzeo

1999 *The NAEP 1998 Reading Report Card for the Nation, NCES 1999-459.* Washington DC: U.S. Department of Education, Office of Educational Research and Improvement, National Center for Education Statistics.

Education Week

1998 *Quality Counts.* 17(17).

Glaser, R., R. Linn, and G. Bohrnstedt

1997 *Assessment in Transition: Monitoring the Nation's Educational Progress.* Stanford, CA: National Academy of Education.

Haney, W., and G.F. Madaus

1991 Cautions on the future of NAEP: Arguments against using NAEP tests and data reporting below the state level. In *Assessing Student Achievement in the States: Background Studies.* Stanford, CA: National Academy of Education.

Haertel, E.H.

1991 Reasonable inferences for the trial state NAEP given the current design: Inferences that can and cannot be made. In *Assessing Student Achievement in the States: Background Studies.* Stanford, CA: National Academy of Education.

Hartka, L., and F. Stancavage

1994 Perspectives on the impact of the 1994 trial state assessments: State assessment directors, state mathematics specialists, and state reading specialists. In *Quality and Utility: The 1994 Trial State Assessment in Reading, Background Studies*. Stanford, CA: National Academy of Education.

Jennings, J., and D. Stark

1997 The future of the National Assessment of Educational Progress. In *Assessment in Transition: Monitoring the Nation's Educational Progress*. Stanford, CA: National Academy of Education.

Johnson, Eugene G.

1994 Standard Errors for Below-State Reporting of National Assessment of Educational Progress, Educational Testing Service. Paper prepared for the National Assessment Governing Board.

Koretz, D.M.

1991 State comparisons using NAEP: Large costs, disappointing benefits. *Educational Researcher* April 19-21.

National Academy of Education

1993 *The Trial State Assessment: Prospects and Realities*, R. Glaser, R. Linn, and G. Bohrnstedt, eds. Panel on the Evaluation of the NAEP Trial State Assessment. Stanford, CA: National Academy of Education.

National Assessment Governing Board

1995a Guidelines for the Conduct of Below-State NAEP Assessments. Policy Statement.

1995b Guidelines for the Conduct of Below-State NAEP Assessments. Draft Implementation Document.

1999 Reporting and Dissemination Committee, Report of August 6.

National Center for Education Statistics

1995a Draft Guidelines and Technical Specifications for the Conduct of Below-State NAEP Assessments.

1995b Technical Specifications for the Conduct of Below-State NAEP Assessments.

National Research Council

1999a *Grading the Nation's Report Card: Evaluating NAEP and Transforming the Assessment of Educational Progress*. Committee on the Evaluation of National and State Assessments of Progress. J.W. Pellegrino, L.R. Jones, and K.M. Mitchell, eds. Commission on Behavioral and Social Sciences and Education. Washington, DC: National Academy Press.

1999b *Embedding Questions: The Pursuit of a Common Measure in Uncommon Tests*. Committee on Embedding Common Test Items in State and District Assessments. D.M. Koretz, M.W. Bertenthal, and B.F. Green, eds. Commission on Behavioral and Social Sciences and Education. Washington, DC: National Academy Press.

1999c *Uncommon Measures: Equivalence and Linkage Among Educational Tests*. Committee on the Equivalency and Linkage of Educational Tests. M.J. Feuer, P.W. Holland, B.F. Green, M.W. Bertenthal, and F.C. Hemphill, eds. Commission on Behavioral and Social Sciences and Education. Washington, DC: National Academy Press.

Olson, J.F., L. Bond, and C. Andrews

In Press *Annual Survey of State Student Assessment Programs: Fall 1998*. Washington, DC: Council of Chief State School Officers.

Roeber, E.D.

1994 Guidelines for the Use of NAEP at the District and School Levels. Paper prepared for the National Assessment Governing Board.

Rust, K.

1999 NAEP Sample Designs and District Level Reporting. Paper prepared for the Workshop on District Level Reporting, September 16.

Selden, R.

1991 The case for district- and school-level results from NAEP. In *Assessing Student Achievement in the States: Background Studies.* Stanford, CA: National Academy of Education.

Shaughnessy, C.A., J.E. Nelson, and N.A. Norris

1997 *NAEP 1996 Mathematics Cross-State Data Compendium for the Grade 4 and Grade 8 Assessment.* Washington DC: National Center for Education Statistics.

Stancavage, F.B., E. Roeber, and G.H. Bohrnstedt

1992 A study of the impact of reporting the results of the 1990 trial state assessment: First report. In *Assessing Student Achievement in the States: Background Studies.* Stanford, CA: National Academy of Education.

1993 Impact of the 1990 trial state assessment: A follow up study. In *The Trial State Assessment: Prospects and Realities: Background Studies.* Stanford, CA: National Academy of Education.

U.S. Department of Education, National Center for Education Statistics

1997 *The NAEP Guide*, NCES 97-900. J. Calderone, L.M. King, and N. Horkay, eds. Washington, DC: U.S. Department of Education.

APPENDIX

A
Workshop on District-Level Reporting for NAEP
Agenda and Participants

Thursday – September 16 Georgetown Suites Hotel

10:00 - 10:15 Welcome and Introductions
Pat DeVito, Chair

10:15 - 12:15 **Panel 1: What purposes would be served by district-level reporting of NAEP?**
Facilitators: LeAnn Gamache and Doug Herrmann

Topics:

a. What information needs might be served?
b. Who would use the results?
c. How would they be used?
d. What are the issues that should be considered?
e. What are the advantages and disadvantages?

SPEAKERS
Wayne Martin, Council of Chief State School Officers
Sharon Lewis, Council of Greater City Schools
Ed Roeber, Advanced Systems in Measurement and Evaluation[a]
Albert Beaton, Boston College[a]

REACTORS
Susan Agruso, South Carolina[b]
Judy Costa, Clark County, Nevada

12:15- 1:15 Lunch

1:15 - 3:15 **Panel 2: What are the implications of district-level reporting for state/local policy, instruction, and assessment?**
Facilitators: Melody Carswell and Lou Fabrizio[b]

Topics:
a. What lessons did states learn from the introduction of state NAEP that help us think about the likely impact of district-level NAEP?
b. What have been the impacts on:
- state testing/education policies,
- state testing programs,
- school curricula,
- schools, teachers, children

c. What types of comparisons are being made?
d. How do the comparisons affect interpretations of state/local testing results?
e. What happens when NAEP results and state/local assessment results differ?

SPEAKERS
Don Watson, Colorado
Bob Silverman, Washington[a]
Peter Behuniak, Connecticut
Susan Agruso, South Carolina[b]

REACTOR
Steve Dunbar, University of Iowa

3:15 – 3:30 Break

3:30 Closed meeting for committee members

Friday – September 17, NAS, Foundry, Room 2004

8:30 - 9:00 Continental breakfast

9:00 – 2:00 **Welcome and Introductions**
Pat DeVito, Chair

Panel 3: To what extent are states and districts interested in district-level reporting? What factors influence their interest?

Topics:
a. What information might district-level reporting provide to you? What information might it provide that is not available from other sources?
b. How might district-level reports be used? What, if any, decisions might be based on reported results?
c. What are the implications of district-level reporting for your state and/or local assessment programs?
d. What lessons from past forays/experiences, if any, with district level reporting of NAEP apply to current context?
e. What factors would influence your interest in future participation in district-level NAEP? (costs, testing burden, reporting schedule, type of reports, possible score uses)
f. Should states and/or districts make decisions about participation in district NAEP?
g. Who should receive the scores? Who should make decisions about score release?

9:00 – 10:45 **Naturally Occurring Districts**
Facilitators: Pat DeVito, Maryellen Donahue

PANEL 3A: SPEAKERS
Carol Perlman, Chicago
Carmen Chapman, Illinois[a]

PANEL 3B: SPEAKERS
Judy Costa, Clark County, Nevada
Tom McIntosh, Nevada

PANEL 3C: SPEAKERS
Robert Tobias, New York City[b]
Gerald DeMauro, New York[a]

10:45 - 11:00 Break

11:00 – 12:00 **Other Interested Districts**
Facilitators: Linda Bryant and Lou Fabrizio[b]

PANEL 3D: SPEAKERS
Paul Cieslak, Milwaukee[c]
Nancy Amuleru-Marshall, Atlanta[a]
Harry Selig, Houston Independent School District
Paula Mosley, Los Angeles Unified School District
Mitchell Chester, Philadelphia

12:00 - 1:00 Lunch

1:00 – 2:00 **PANEL 3D, CONTINUED**

2:00 - 3:30 **Panel 4: Technical and Policy Issues**
Facilitators: Audrey Qualls and Duane Steffey

Topics:
Issues related to sampling and administration
Issues related to reporting of scores and conditioning
Issues related to policy

- What constitutes a district?
- Who makes participation decisions?
- Who "owns" the data?
- Who gets to see and use the data?

PANELISTS
Rick Vallient, Westat
Nancy Allen, ETS[a]
Peggy Carr, NCES
Roy Truby, NAGB

REACTOR
Lauress Wise, HumRRO

3:30 **Adjourn**

***

PARTICIPANTS

Nancy Allen,[a] Director, NAEP Analysis and Research, Educational Testing Service
Nancy Amuleru-Marshall,[a] Executive Director, Research and Assessment, Atlanta Public Schools
Al Beaton,[a] Professor, Educational Evaluation, School of Education, Boston College
Peter Behuniak, Director of Student Assessment and Testing, Connecticut State Department of Education
Peggy Carr, Associate Commissioner, Assessment Division, National Center for Education Statistics, U.S. Department of Education
Carmen Chapman,[a] Administrator, Division of Assessment, Illinois State Department of Education
Mitchell Chester, Executive Director, Office of Accountability and Assessment, School District of Philadelphia
Paul Cieslak,[c] Research Specialist, Milwaukee Public Schools
Judy Costa, Testing Director, Clark County School District, Las Vegas, NV

Gerald DeMauro,[a] Coordinator of Assessment, Office of State Assessment, Albany, NY
Steve Dunbar, Professor of Educational Measurement and Statistics, College of Education, The University of Iowa
Sharon Lewis, Director of Research, Council of the Great City Schools
Wayne Martin, Director, State Education Assessment Center, Council of Chief State School Officers
Thomas McIntosh, Team Leader, Nevada Department of Education
Paula Mosley, Coordinator, Student Testing and Evaluation, Office of Instruction, Los Angeles, CA
Carole L. Perlman, Director of Student Assessment, Chicago Public Schools
Edward Roeber,[a] Vice President of External Relations, Advanced Systems in Measurement and Evaluation, Dover, NH
Harry Selig, Research Manager, Research and Accountability Department, Houston Independent School District, Houston, TX
Robert Silverman,[a] Senior Analyst for Assessment, Olympia, WA
Roy Truby, Executive Director, National Assessment Governing Board
Richard Valliant, Associate Director, Statistical Group, WESTAT
Don Watson, Acting Director, Student Assessment, Colorado Department of Education
Lauress L. Wise, President, Human Resources Research Organization

---

Hurricane Floyd interfered with participants' travel plans:
[a]Participated via speaker phone for a portion of the meeting
[b]Unable to attend
[c]Provided written comments but did not participate

APPENDIX B
Background Information on NAEP

The National Assessment of Educational Progress (NAEP) has been assessing students across the country since 1969, providing valuable information about students' performance in various content domains. Results of the national assessment, frequently called "the nation's report card," were presented annually from 1969 to 1979. Since 1980, national NAEP has been administered every two years, with the implementation of a state-level NAEP system in 1990.

PURPOSES

Since its beginning, NAEP has served as a barometer of student academic performance across the country. It provides data on trends in the academic performance of elementary, middle, and secondary students in key subject areas and has proven to be a unique source of background information that has both informed and guided educational policy. NAEP results have the credence and power to inform and guide educational policy largely due to the integrity with which NAEP is viewed. The results are used to (National Research Council 1999a: 27):

- describe the status of the education system,
- describe the performance of students in different demographic groups,

- identify the knowledge and skills over which students have (or do not have) mastery,
- support judgments about the adequacy of observed performance,
- argue the success or failure of instructional content and strategies,
- discuss relationships among achievement and school and family variables,
- reinforce the call for high academic standards and education reform, and
- argue for system and school accountability.

NAEP is considered by education stakeholders at various local, state, and national levels to be the national benchmark[1] of both content and performance standards and to provide valuable information for national and state comparisons. For each of the content areas, NAGB has developed an organizing framework. The NAEP frameworks—derived from a national consensus process that includes educators, policy makers, practitioners, and scholars in the respective fields—denote the broadly accepted content standards that students in fourth, eighth, and twelfth grades should seek to attain. The released items give examples of the kind of questions and level of content knowledge assessed at each grade.

INDICATORS OF ACHIEVEMENT

NAEP assesses a vast array of content areas. Due to the many content areas and the need to limit the length of the testing time, a matrix sampling design is used to obtain a representative sample of students taking each subject-area assessment. Under this design, blocks of items within each content domain are administered to groups of students, making it possible to administer a large number and range of items during a relatively brief testing period. Consequently, each student takes only a few items in a content domain. As a result, the performance of any particular student cannot be accurately measured, preventing achievement scores for individual students from being available. NAEP, thus, reports only group-level results.

NAEP subject-matter achievement is reported through scale scores.

[1] "Benchmarking" means measuring one's own practices against those of others, and, in this context, refers to the practice of comparing local or state-level test results against those derived from national indicators.

Scale scores summarize student performance (on a scale of 0-500) in a given subject area for the nation as a whole and for subsets of the population based on demographic and background characteristics. Results are tabulated over time to provide trend information.

Academic achievement is also summarized using performance standards, or achievement levels. NAGB has established policy definitions for three levels of student achievement—basic, proficient, and advanced (U.S. Department of Education, 1997). The achievement levels denote the range of performance established for each grade and describe the levels of knowledge demonstrated by students:

> *Basic*: partial mastery of prerequisite knowledge and skills that are fundamental for proficient work at each grade.
>
> *Proficient*: solid academic performance for each grade assessed. Students reaching this level have demonstrated competency over challenging subject matter, including subject-matter knowledge, application of such knowledge to real-world situations, and analytical skills appropriate to the subject matter.
>
> *Advanced*: superior performance.

There is also a fourth level of student achievement, "below-basic," for which no description is provided.

BACKGROUND, CONTEXTUAL, AND ENVIRONMENTAL INFORMATION

NAEP collects a variety of demographic, background, and contextual information on students, teachers, and administrators. Student demographic information, such as race/ethnicity, gender, and highest level of parental education, are available. As stated above, NAEP summarizes results by certain demographic and educational characteristics.

Contextual and environmental data collected during NAEP administrations provides information in such areas as students' course selection, homework habits, use of textbooks and computers, and communication with parents about schoolwork. Information obtained about teachers pertains to such areas as the kind of training, number of years teaching, and instructional practices. Administrators also respond to questions about their schools, including the location and type of school, school enrollment numbers, and levels of parental involvement.